Suzuki
Piano School
Volume 4

© 1978 Dr. Shinichi Suzuki
Sole publisher for the entire world except Japan:
Summy-Birchard Inc.
exclusively distributed by
Warner Bros. Publications
15800 N.W. 48th Avenue, Miami, Florida 33014
All rights reserved   Printed in U.S.A.

ISBN 0-87487-163-8

INTRODUCTION

FOR THE STUDENT: This material is part of the worldwide Suzuki Method of teaching. Companion recordings should be used with these publications.

FOR THE TEACHER: In order to be an effective Suzuki teacher, a great deal of ongoing education is required. Your national Suzuki association provides this for its membership. Teachers are encouraged to become members of their national Suzuki associations and maintain a teacher training schedule, in order to remain current, via institutes, short-term programs and long-term programs. You are also encouraged to join the International Suzuki Association.

FOR THE PARENT: Credentials are essential for any teacher you choose. We recommend you ask your teacher for his or her credentials, especially those relating to training in the Suzuki Method. The Suzuki Method experience should be a positive one, where there exists a wonderful, fostering relationship between child, parent and teacher. So choosing the right teacher is of the utmost importance.

In order to obtain more information about the Suzuki Method, please contact your country's Suzuki Association; the International Suzuki Association at 3-10-15 Fukashi, Matsumoto City 390, Japan; The Suzuki Association of the Americas, P.O. Box 17310, Boulder, Colorado 80308; or Summy-Birchard Inc., c/o Warner Bros. Publications, 15800 N.W. 48th Avenue, Miami, Florida 33014, for current Associations' addresses.

CONTENTS

1
Rondo
ロンド

W. A. Mozart
モーツァルト

2
Minuet I
from 8 Minuets with Trio

メヌエット 1

W. A. Mozart
モーツァルト

Menuet I des 8 Menuets avec Trio

Menuett I aus 8 Menuette mit Trio Minué I de Ocho Minués con Trio

Trio

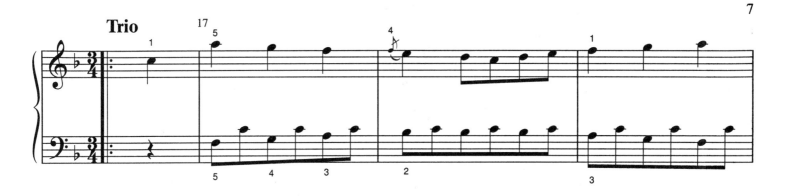

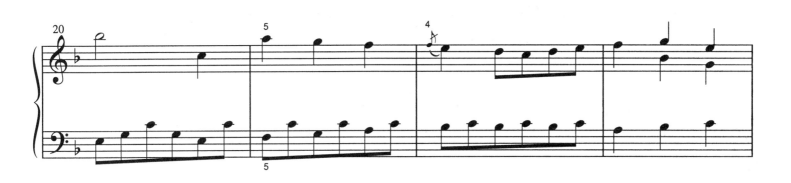

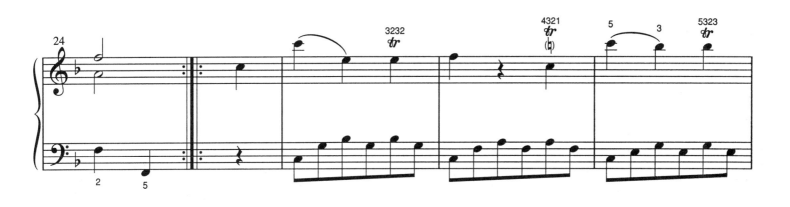

Minuet da capo

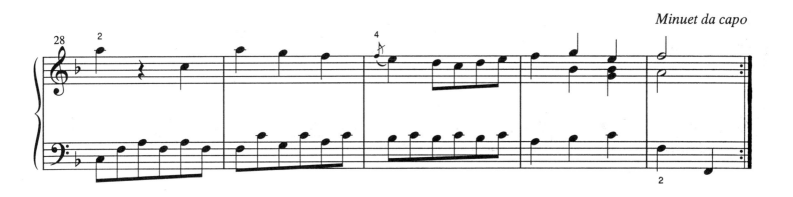

3
Minuet III
from 8 Minuets with Trio

メヌエット 3

W. A. Mozart
モーツァルト

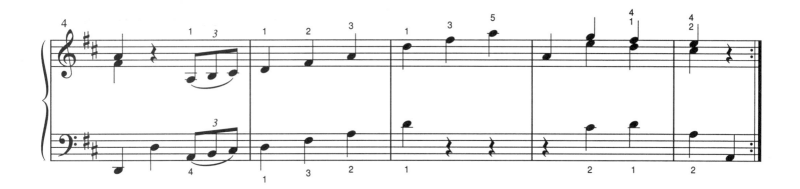

Menuet III des 8 Menuets avec Trio

Menuett III aus 8 Menuette mit Trio   Minué III de Ocho Minués con Trío

Trio

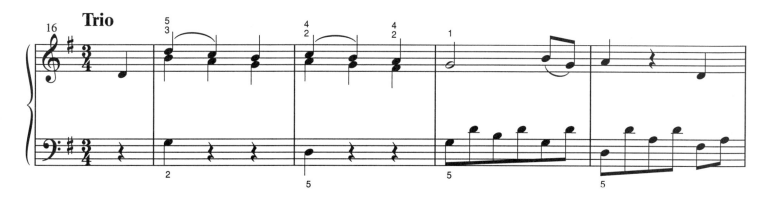

Minuet da capo

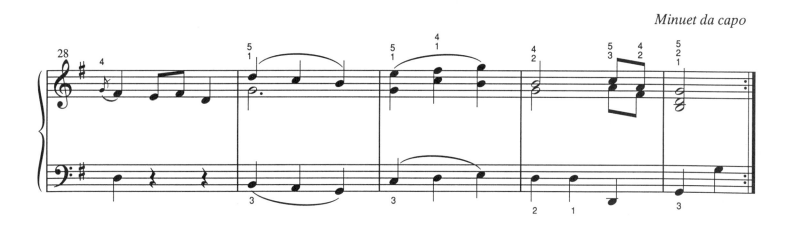

4
Minuet VIII
from 8 Minuets with Trio

メヌエット 8

W. A. Mozart
モーツァルト

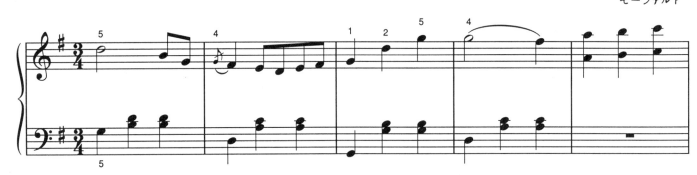

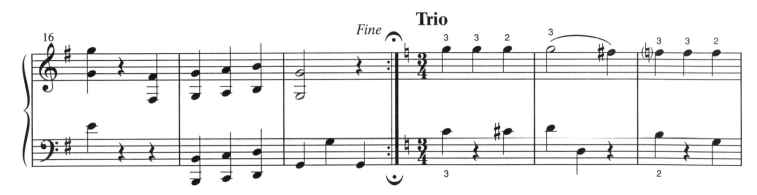

Menuet VIII des 8 menuets avec Trio

Menuett VIII aus 8 Menuette mit Trio   Minué VIII de Ocho Minués con Trío

Minuet da capo

5
Musette
ミュゼット

J. S. Bach
バッハ

Allegro con brio

This page has been left blank to facilitate page turns.

6
Sonata
Op. 49, No. 2
ソナタ

L. van Beethoven
ベートーベン

Allegro, ma non troppo

Sonate, Op, 49, No, 2   *Sonate, Op. 49, Nr. 2*   Sonata, Op. 49, No. 2

Tempo di minuetto

7
Gavotte
ガボット

J. S. Bach
バッハ

8
Minuet I
from Partita in B♭

メヌエット　1

J. S. Bach
バッハ

Menuet de la Partita en si bémol　　　***Menuett aus Partita in B***　　　*Minué de Partitura en si bemol*

Minuet II
メヌエット　2

Minuet I da capo

9

Gigue
from Partita in B♭

ジーグ

J. S. Bach
バッハ

Gigue de la Partita en si bémol　　*Gigue aus Partita in B*　　Gigue de Partitura en si bemol